nF421427

World War II

Letters To A Brother From Tinian Island
In The Mariana Islands.

L. D. MANERA

KLEMME   5th Sqdn
"Umbriago"

AC	Klemme, Robert E.	1Lt
P	Gaudino, John R.	2Lt
N	Worrel, Vernon J.	2Lt
B	Riley, Vaughn E.	2Lt
B	Dutrow, William	2Lt
FE	Hill, Robert T.	TSgt
RN	Hauenstein, William D.	Sgt
RO	Tomaszewski, Chester C.	Sgt
CFC	Sikes, Benjamin G.	Sgt
RG	Breen, Dennis F.	Sgt
LG	Kerr, John R.	SSgt
TG	Zobrist, Howard T.	Sgt
CC	Komarek, Harold F.	SSgt

Rear: Worrel, Gaudino, Klemme, Riley, & Hill.
Front: Breen, Tomaszewski, Sikes, Hauenstein,
Kerr, & Zobrist.

Copyright

FORWARD

These handwritten letters are from John Russell (Russ) Kerr to his oldest brother, Robert (Bob) Kerr. Here is a biography of Russ taken from 9th Bombardment Group (VH) HISTORY (1st, 5th, and 99th Squadrons, p. 341)

> *JOHN R. KERR: Born near Lima, OH, 1917, and graduated from Harrod High School in 1935. Married Arnita in 1942 and drafted into the army Nov. 10, 1943. While in basic training volunteered from the Army Air Force and completed gunnery school. Assigned to Robert Klemme's crew in McCook as left gunner on the "Umbriago." Flew 35 missions. Discharged from service in 1945 and returned to employment at Lima Westinghouse Aerospace Division. Graduated with a MBA degree. At Westinghouse worked on the electrical system as an engineer for the Apollo Spacecraft that placed the first man on the moon. Retired in 1981, worked as a consultant for five years and am now enjoying traveling and golf. My wife has been very supportive in my endeavors and has helped put our two children through college.*

Russ is writing these letters from Tinian Island where he is stationed off the Mariana Islands near Japan. Russ is a Left Gunner of the "Umbriago". The Airplane Commander is Robert E. Klemme. The 5th Squadron is under Lt. Col. Malvern Brown who reports to Col. Henry C. Huglin of the 9th Bombardment Group.

Bob received these letters when he lived on Annabelle Street in Detroit, Michigan. After Bob moved to his home in Allen Park, Michigan, there was a flood in the basement where these letters got wet and got water damaged. A few letters are very difficult to read. I humbly compile these letters for future kin and those interested in the time of World War II. I leave the original spellings, punctuation, and phrases.

While reading these letters, there is mention of missions. I located these missions and inserted them in a separate section. I realized there was a lot of information in Russ's letters about the entertainment world such as movies, live entertainment; and baseball players. This information is included at the end of each letter.

TABLE OF CONTENTS

Letters From Russ Kerr To Bob Kerr

The Neil House
across from the capitol
Columbus Ohio
Nov. 21, 1943

Hello folks,

At the moment I am rather happy, because Arnita and Ronda Lou
are with me. I have a weekend pass and we are staying at this hotel.
Arnita brought two other ladies with her so they could see their
husbands and do a little loving – you know how that is (Ha). We have
been doing our share of loving also (ha).

After taking and passing about 5 or 6 tests I finally landed in the Air
Corps. And I'm waiting to be shipped out. It's a tough branch to get
into, but by studying hard I made it O.K.

You should have seen Ronda when she first saw me. She held out her
arms and I picked her up, she said "daddy, daddy," then she would
pat me with her hands and love me. She sure is a swell kid. I was on
duty as a military policeman Fri. nite and this helped to get my
weekend pass.\

I don't know for sure yet, but I believe I will be sent to some College
for my studying after I've had my basic training. So I'll give you my
address when I get stationed then you can write to me.

I suppose Bob can still hit the bullseye with those darts, but someday
I may be able to beat him.

In closing, I hope you folks are all O.K. and write to me when I get
stationed.

Your Brother,
Russ

Cpl. John R. Kerr 35294052
5th Squad 9th Bomb. Grp
A.P.O. 247 c/o Postmaster
San Francisco, Calif.
January 29, 1945

Dear Brother & Family:

I'm sure by now you all are wondering where I am. Well you can put your minds at ease now as I have arrived at my overseas destination safe and sound without any trouble at all. I didn't know there was so much water in the Pacific Ocean. I can reveal that I am somewhere in the Mariana group of islands and that is all. There still are a few japs left on the island and they generally let the Marines go Jap hunting on their day off just for the pleasure of it (Ha).

Anyway, I carry my "45" revolver with me at all times just in case someone doesn't want to borrow it. Souvenir hunting is strictly forbidden because of booby traps which is very logical.

The weather here is rather warm, but the breezes from the ocean are nice and cool. I just wear shorts most of the time.

For recreation I generally play horseshoe and softball. I suppose your bowling average is among the best by now, Bob.

Arnita and Ronda came to see me in Kansas a few days before I left. Ronda sure thinks her daddy is all right. Maybe this spring they can come to see you folks for a short stay. Arnita told me that since she has been driving all over the States, Detroit is only a short distance (ha).

How's the young ladies' getting along with their school work? I suppose Sally is still performing under the lights. I suppose also that G. Lou is looking after the boys.

Later on I may be able to tell you more about my work, but at present censorship rules do not allow me to.

Will close now and write more later and I hope everybody is well and
O.K.

Your Brother,
Russ

P.S. Don't forget to write.

Cpl. John R. Kerr 35294052
5th Squad 9th Bomb. Grp
A.P.O. 247 c/o Postmaster
San Francisco, Calif.
February 10, 1945
Saturday, 9:30 P.M.

Dear Brother & Family,

I received your letters yesterday and was really glad to hear from you. They were sent here from Herington. I was surprised that G. Lou could write such nice letters. So I'll answer both letters in one if G. Lou will let me (ha). Glad to hear that you are still going good with your bowling, Bob, so keep it up. The lights just went out so I'll finish this by flashlight.

The Seabees around here sure do work hard and fast and they sure deserve a lot of credit. I've been getting letters in bunches from Arnita, but none have as yet been sent to my permanent A.P.O. number, but to my temporary number in California. Arnita writes that her and Ronda are getting along good and that's what I like to hear from home. I talked to Arnita over the telephone before I left the States and also to Ronda. Ronda could hear me alright, but she was too excited to say anything. She sure is a pill. I called Mom and Dad first in the morning and told them to have Arnita and Ronda there in the evening so everything worked out swell.

There still picking off a Jap now and then that are holed up here in caves. We are guarded good at nights so I guess I sleep pretty peacefully.

[Letter cut out] things are just about the same around here. The weather is nice and cool this evening so I'll get a good nights rest - I hope.

Arnita has a large picture of our crew and maybe, if you mention it, she would get one reproduced for you folks. I wish you could get one and I think we have a swell crew. There all good boys to work with.

Ronda can pick me out in the picture every time. She sure thinks her daddy is just it.

I hope this letter is as interesting to you folks as much as I have tried to make it so. It's about the same thing every day, and with censorship and all, it is hard to write about things you would like to say most.

I write to Arnita every day, of course, and this makes my 5th letter today. Tell the girls I said hello – listen at me say tell them – I'll bet they read this first (ha). I also received letters from Dad and Mom, Henry's and Lyman's yesterday. It sure makes me feel good to get all that mail.

Well, I guess that's about all I know at present, so I'll sign off now till next time.

Your Brother,
Russ

Sgt. John R. Kerr 35294052
5th Squad 9th Bomb. Grp
A.P.O. 247 c/o Postmaster
San Francisco, Calif.
February 27, 1945
Tuesday, 9 A.M.

Dear Brother and Family,

I'm in the writing mood this morning so watch out – here I go (ha). I just finished a letter to Mom and Dad and I thought I had better write to you folks also as I haven't heard from you for quite a while. In order to write any volume in a letter, I have to just concentrate on happenings in my own immediate area and what I am doing. The bigger things of course are still military information and cannot be divulged at present. So you see practically all letters that I write back home are just the same with one exception and that is those letters to my wife, which I'm sure, would be embarrassing to anyone else (ha).

Anyway, I'm feeling fine and getting plenty to eat. About a week ago the PX had beer for the first time and I might say those five cans of beer tasted pretty good even tho they were rather warm. Until recently I had to conserve on my writing paper, but the PX got some in and now it won't be so bad.

Arnita sent me a picture of the cattle Dad has been feeding which was in the Lima News. Schoonover sold them to the Lima Packing Co. and they claimed they were the best beef that they had bought. Dad had a little write up also and I'm sure he is mighty proud of that. By the way, did you ever get those films developed that you took of those cattle and of me? It was rather dark that day and I hope they turned out O.K.

Tomorrow is pay day and I am looking forward to that as it will be my first pay since I have been here. I really don't know what I would spend it on though, so I'll probably send it all home. Arnita writes that she and Ronda and Grandma Baier are getting along fine, which I am glad to hear. She said Ronda took a tour of our basement the other day for the first time and naturally Arnita had a job on her hands besides trying to do her washing (ha). Ronda takes my picture to bed with her every nite and anybody that visits there, Ronda has to tell them all about daddy. I think Arnita and Ronda are planning on coming to see you folks as soon as it gets a little warmer.

The weather here is as usual – warm and I am getting a swell tan out of it. I understand they had lots of snow back home which seems rather odd to me since it is so nice and warm here. Well, it is just about time for P.T., so I'll finish this letter later.

Just got through playing volleyball for my P.T. and had a lot of fun. Our co-pilot is good at any kind of sports. He really puts me in mind of Paul a lot as he is tall and looks something like him. The folks say that Paul is a German prisoner of war and I'm hoping he is well and O.K. I think I know already what he has been through.

Is Detroit still the same old busy city? I've been wondering, Bob, how your bowling has been holding up? How are the girls getting along in school? I'll bet they're looking forward to their summer vacation already. Probably after a while I can reveal exactly where I am at in the Mariannas, but not as yet. Last nite I saw a swell show "Shine on Harvest Moon" with Anne Sheridan. Our crew generally goes every nite with our stools and boxes to sit on unless we get into a hot card game (ha). Well, folks, I'll be signing off for now and I hope this letter finds everybody well, so write.

Your Bro,
Russ

Sgt. John R. Kerr 35294052
5th Squad 9th Bomb. Grp
A.P.O. 247 c/o Postmaster
San Francisco, Calif.
March 1, 1945
Friday, 9:30 P.M.

Dear Bob and Family,

Just heard from Arnita that Sally was quite sick with strep throat and
I am hoping that she is well by now. Lyman wrote that Fred Kirts
(from Alger) had died of a heart attack. He also wanted to know all
about my work and how I was getting along. Inquisitive wasn't he
(Ha)?

You folks are also probably wondering by now. Recently, I was on a
Tokyo mission for my first trip there. It was too cloudy for me to see
this big town so all I can say is that I've been over it but not yet have
I saw it (ha). You all probably read about the raid in your papers and
I'm sure they didn't have to kindle any fires for their dinner that
night.

It was a long ride and rather tiresome as we were in the air about 15
hours. One of our ships had a little trouble and it took them 18 hours
which set some kind of a new record. Anyway we sure knew when
we were over the city even though we couldn't see Tokyo.

Well, I suppose your snow is all melted by now and your waiting in
some warm weather and here I am over here waiting on cooler
weather (ha). We now have 3 more boys in our tent from a new crew,
which makes us a tent full.

Did I tell you that I had a moustache and a short haircut? Well, I
have (ha). I sure wish you folks could send me some of your pictures
and maybe I can send some of me. The lights just went out on me
and I'm finishing this by flashlight so I'll hurry it up. Arnita writes
that Ronda is still up and coming and on the go all the time.

3 of our crew are on airplane guard tonite and I went to the show. We all played cards today and of course I had a lucky streak (ha). Yes quite lucky. Well, Bob, how is your work holding out? I guess Lyman is working nites again. I had better be signing off now so I can hit the sack for the night as it is a cool nite to sleep. We get beer tomorrow again and a bottle of coke. I took a can of beer along on the Tokyo mission and it was ice cold when we got back. Well don't work too hard and write.

Your Brother,
Russ

5th Squad 9th Bomb. Grp
A.P.O. 247 c/o Postmaster
San Francisco, Calif.
March 7, 1945
Wednesday, 9 P.M.

Dear Bro Bob and Family,

Received a letter today from you folks dated February 19th, so I'm writing right back in answer to it. This is the 2nd one of your letters so far and as a suggestion I wish you could send your letters airmail as it only takes from 7 to 10 days for them to get here. Ha. Right now the boys are telling stories and I think I'll have to roll up my pant legs. Anyway I sort of forgotten what I had wrote you before, so bear with me if I repeat anything I have written before. I had pancakes for breakfast this morning and liver for supper tonite.

I don't know whether I told you about our last mission or not, but we lone wolfed it over the Empire and back. It only took us 13 hours which is some sort of a record. Yes, Bob, I think we are (as you say) making meat out of those Japs and I think the newspapers can tell you better than I.

Glad to hear that those pictures came out so good so save them. That sure sounds good about turning out more planes as that will, I'm sure, shorten the war considerable.

I imagine your team is still in the lead yet with about 6 more weeks to go by now. We played another crew a game of softball the other day for our P.T. period. I pitched and our Bombardier caught. We beat them 9 to 1. By the way, our Bombardier is from Ft. Wayne.

I didn't attend the movie tonite as it was something I saw before, so stayed here and wrote letters. Your letter was the only one today, but Arnita's last letter was dated February 25th and that isn't bad mail service. I understand we will soon have some pictures taken of our crew here and if possible at all I'll send you one.

How are the girls getting along in school by now? Tell everybody hello for me and maybe some day we can all get together for a shindig. Bernice, I received a Xmas card from your folks and I don't believe I ever wrote them about it so if you will please thank them for remembering us.

The weather here is still about the same except it poured down rain this evening and it will be a nice nite to sleep. I now have an air cushion mattress to sleep on. Ernie Pyle has been writing about the Mariana group of Islands. If he writes for your paper – read it, as it is quite interesting.

Well folks, I'll close for the present until next time, so don't work too hard. By the way our Radar Operator is from Lansing and a good boy. Write.

Your Bro.
Russ

P.S. Arnita is still planning on coming to see you.

Sgt. John R. Kerr 35294052
5th Squad 9th Bomb. Grp
A.P.O. 247c/o Postmaster
San Francisco, Calif.
March 18, 1945
Sunday 5:30 P.M.

Dear Brother and Family,

Received your letter today – Feb. 8th was the date on it and it seems it was a little late in coming. My airmail generally gets here within 7 – 10 days. Anyway I was sure glad to hear from you folks so I'm answering right away while I have the time. We've been kept pretty busy lately and I haven't hardly had time to write to Arnita. I guess I have been on several missions since I last wrote. Our crew now have 7 to their credit. On our last one we went through a cloud of smoke over the target and the turbulence and heat slung us around like jelly beans. (Ha) My head hit the top of the ship like popcorn popping over a hot fire. Otherwise we had no trouble whatever and had excellent bombing results.

I hear the newspapers are talking up our work over here and boy I sure have seen many, many fires. I saw some of the big league ballplayers playing here this afternoon. Vander Meer pitched for one of the many teams. Everybody was taking pictures and autographs right and left.

Well folks, I'll sign off for now, so don't work too hard and I'll write later.

Your Bro,
Russ

Johnny Vander Meer

(Article from Cincinnati.com)

Sgt. John R. Kerr 35294052
5th Squad 9th Bomb. Grp
A.P.O. 247c/o Postmaster
San Francisco, Calif.
March 28, 1945
Thursday 12:30 P.M.

Dear Bro & Family,

Boy-o-boy your letters are now piling up on me so I'll have to get busy and write back. Your last letter only took 7 days to get here and that's not bad. In fact I haven't had time to write much lately as I've been quite busy.

Georganna wrote quite an interesting letter also. She has the right idea about us going over the Empire, but we try not to think of those things. We have a job to do and it has to be done. About our crew's picture, Georganna, I think Arnita intends to bring it when she comes for a visit and maybe Betty will come along. Thanks for the picture, G. Lou, that sure is a swell picture. Bob, that 200 average bowling game must have been rather exciting. That's some score.

Bernice, we have an outside theatre here with a nice stage and if you could bring your Rising Stars over here some evening for a show everybody would sure appreciate it. Seriously though we did have a stage show put on by the Civilians here the other night. Some of them were Japs, Koreans, and another group, but they all look alike to me. Of course I couldn't understand them and their songs and dances were very primitive. None of them are over 5 ft. tall, but they sure are quick. Glad you got to see some news reels of the fight at Iwo Jima. Those Marines sure had a rough time there and I should know as I have already talked to some of them and I have also seen the results.

I can imagine the time you are having with those negroes now since they are all making big money. Next thing they will be trying to run the town. So I don't blame you for trying to keep them out of your community.

The weather here is still about the same sunshine – rain – sunshine – rain, etc. We are still living in our tent, but our new barracks will soon be up and we will have better quarters. Otherwise, we have plenty of cigarettes, cigars, candy bars, gum, etc. so it isn't too bad.

Arnita is sending me lots of reading material, especially those small pocket books. Ronda is still up and coming and likes to be outdoors. She says she likes everybody "two bushels" (ha). Well folks, I guess that's about all for now, so I'll close and will write later. Write soon.

As ever, Your Bro,
Russ

P.S. Our crew now has 8 missions to is credit.

Sgt. John R. Kerr 35294052
5th Squad 9th Bomb. Grp
A.P.O. 247 c/o Postmaster
San Francisco, Calif.
April 5, 1945
Thursday, 7 P.M.

Dear Bro. & Family,

Hello everybody. How are you all? I haven't received a letter now for
3 days now and I thought I had better keep writing to everybody so
I'll get lots of letters later (ha). I think that maybe the weather is
holding our mail up though. It was really hot today and no rain for a
change. We oiled and cleaned our guns this afternoon. Played
checkers this morning – I guess I'm getting to be quite a checker
player now. I played some gin rummy this afternoon which I just
learned to play. I played softball yesterday with our squadron team
and we beat 5 – 0. I played shortshop. Keep letting me know, Bob,
about your bowling as I'm betting on your team. Sometimes we have
a lot of time out around here and sometimes we don't

We have pulled 3 missions in one week. Our crew now has 9
missions to its credit. I saw our latest crew picture today that was
taken here before a mission and I'll send you one if at all possible.
Well folks, I'll close for now and I hope everybody is O.K.

As ever, Your Bro.
Russ

Sgt. John R. Kerr 35294052
5th Squad 9th Bomb. Grp
A.P.O. 247 c/o Postmaster
San Francisco, Calif.
April 7, 1945
Saturday, 7 P.M.

Dear Bro & Family,

Received your letter yesterday night after I wrote, so will answer again. The last 3 days sure has been hot, but it is cooler this evening. My mail is still being held up for some reason or other and one of these days I'll probably get about forty eleven letters. Lyman says he is mowing the lawn and planting garden. Arnita, Ronda, Betty and the folks were at his place March 25 for their anniversary and Janice's 3rd birthday. Glad to hear your still leading the league. The folks are getting along O.K. In fact Dad has gained 10 lbs.

Oh yes we're having our first U.S.O. show tonite and some of our boys have been there for 1 hour now and it doesn't start till 9. That will make 3 more hrs to wait (Lou). So I'm writing letters till then. I'll tell you about it later. Well, Bob, we were rather unlucky on our last attempt for a mission as we had to turn back a short distance out. We had to feather an engine. Hope we have better luck next time. I'll close now and I sure appreciate you writing soon.

As Ever, Your Bro,
Russ

Sgt. John R. Kerr 35294052
5th Squad 9th Bomb. Grp
A.P.O. 247 c/o Postmaster
San Francisco, Calif.
April 9, 1945
Monday, 12:30 P.M.

Dear Bob & Family,

Received your letter yesterday dated Mar 30 and also one from
everybody else. Everybody is well and feeling O.K. Henry is having
some new front teeth put in and they are remodeling their kitchen.
Dad is rebuilding one of Tom's barns and sowing oats. Mom said dad
was taking things a little easier now and not working so hard. There
driving the station wagon more. Sure wish I were there to drive one
of those tractors. I went to church yesterday and played ball in the
afternoon.

Say, when your team wins that bowling league trophy, I'll be
expecting a cigar you know. Glad to hear Sally is doing as good with
her shows and I'll write G. Lou a letter also when I receive hers. That
will make her feel better, I'm sure, since she has wrote so often.

Yes, Ronda must be growing up and I sure wish I could see her, but
Arnita is going to send me some pictures of them. Lyman said they
wanted to come see you folks also, but Evelyn wasn't in "shape" - ??
Well, I'll close for now and I'll write later. We haven't done any flying
lately. Don't work too hard.

Your Bro.
Russ

Sgt. John R. Kerr 35294052
5th Squad 9th Bomb. Grp
A.P.O. 247 c/o Postmaster
San Francisco, Calif.
April 15, 1945
Sunday 1 P.M.

Dear Bro. Bob & Family,

Received your letter yesterday dated Apr 6th and sure glad to hear from you. I also received the Lima News and a letter from Arnita. Sure felt good to read the old home-town newspaper even though it was a month old. Arnita wrote that our neighbors in the other side of the house have moved and she had quite a time with prospective renters (ha). She sure was glad that they moved and so was I as she already promised it to someone she knew before. It's a cousin of her girlfriend from Dola. Then a while ago I received 4 letters from Arnita and one from Lyman.

They were rather worried about me as they hadn't heard from me for several days and Lyman said he heard of several B-29s being knocked down over the target, but my mail came through then and they were quite relieved. I think the weather held our mail up both ways during that time.

Arnita has been quite busy now cleaning up the other part of the house and also doing her own spring housecleaning. Of course Ronda is also right in the middle of things and I do hope they can come to see you folks real soon.

Arnita saw Margaret in town last week and she had just given a pt. of blood for the Red Cross.

Right now I'm studying this bowling league form and who are these boys – A. Roberts and G. Roberts? It looks like they have the best individual average of all the players in all the leagues. This fellow G. Roberts must be good and your lucky to have him don't you think? Anyway you probably have won your league by now and I sure would like to be there for those doubles, especially since the beer is free (ha). Tell Sally that I sure wished she would dedicate a dance for me even though I'm not in Detroit, I sure would appreciate it. Then you can write and tell me about it. Tell G. Lou I showed her picture to some of our youngsters here and they like it.

Today at noon we had 5 min. of silence for your late President Roosevelt. In our Church, Services also today was mostly about Roosevelt and for our new leader – Truman. Yesterday they published on the bulletin board our authority to have the Air Medal from the period of Feb. 3 to Mar 13th for bravery etc. Well I guess that's about all I know at present, so write and I hope you are all okay.

Love,
Russ

P.S. It might interest you to know that we now have 10 missions in.

Death of President Roosevelt
(New York Times)

The Air Medal (AM) is a military decoration of the United States Armed Forces. It was created in 1942 and is awarded for single acts of heroism or meritorious achievement while participating in aerial flight.

(amcmuseum.org)

Sgt. John R. Kerr 35294052
5th Squad 9th Bomb. Grp
A.P.O. 247 c/o Postmaster
San Francisco, Calif.
April 19, 1945
Thursday, 1 P.M.

Dear Bob & Family,

I have now before me your letter postmarked Apr. 12 and I think you
got your dates mixed as your letter was dated Apr 13th (Ha) I
sounded like some lawyer on that didn't I? Anyway I sure appreciate
your writing so often and that is the reason I answer as soon. I also
received 2 more letters from Arnita today. I'll find time to answer all
my mail if I have to sit up nites doing it (ha). I have already wrote to
Lyman and the folks back home this forenoon. Mom said that Ronda
likes to follow Dad around every place he goes and she also likes to
sit on his lap. She calls him "paw –paw" and she wants to be
outdoors all the time. I can imagine what a time she would have with
her daddy right now. Arnita had Ronda her pictures taken and she is
going to send me one soon. Since her daddy can't be with her at
present, I am glad that she is able to be contented all the time. I
received some good pocket books from Arnita the other day and
now I have plenty of reading material.

Since we have moved into our new barracks, we have things much
nicer, in fact, practically all the conveniences that we had in the
States. We have a big barrel on the back porch with a smaller barrel
inside it. Sawdust is packed around the smaller one in which we keep
our ice for ice cold beer and we also keep our canteens there for cold
water. I only have a coke in it now as my beer doesn't last too long
(ha). But I'll drink a cold beer today on your success as champs of the
Maples. You sure ended up strong. Have you quit playing softball?

The boys just told me that we now have a new B-29 to fly. Guess we
will have to call it Umbringo II as that was the name of our other
one. We now have 11 missions in and, as you say, things are tough,

because everybody doesn't get back on some missions. Today is a nice day with a nice breeze blowing. I guess that's about all I know at present except Arnita wrote that Betty was awarded the Air Medal in Ft. Wayne recently. You get the Air Medal for your first mission and then cluster for every five. I'll sign off now till next time.

Your Bro,
Russ

Sgt. John R. Kerr 35294052
5th Squad 9th Bomb. Grp
A.P.O. 247 c/o Postmaster
San Francisco, Calif.
April 28, 1945
Saturday, 11 A.M.

Dear Bob & Family,

Well here I am again getting behind on my letters. I received your letter dated April 19th day before yesterday and am just finding time to answer it. I also received G. Lou's letter too and I'll answer it on a V-Mail which will be something new for her I think unless she has other boyfriends in the service (ha). Bob you forgot to tell me what your amount of money came to for the bowling prize, but Georgeanna didn't forget (ha). I might send you some pineapple plants and fir trees and banana trees for your front yard. Or some palm trees – which do you prefer? I can get plenty of beer here, but when you talk about hot dogs why that's something different.

Well folks we had a big parade the other day and Gen. Davies handed out the medals which included the Bronze Star, Silver Star, Purple Heart, Distinguished Flying Cross, Oak Leave Cluster, and Air Medals. Our crew all got the Air Medal and got to shake hands with the General after he pinned our medal on. I am sending my medal home today.

Recently we completed our 12th mission and it was our first encounter with Jap fighters. I got a few bursts at them but they kept their distance when they saw the bullets flying at them. They were actually out of range and that's where I would rather keep them (ha). Well, so much for that. It sounds like Germany is practically defeated – I hope. The night before our last mission we tried to take off and only got half way down the runway when 2 engines cut out on us, so we came back in and went to bed. But on our last mission we broke in our new ship and everything worked swell.

Well, Bob, I guess that's about all I know at present. Arnita has been painting our bathroom and Ronda has been helping (ha). So I'll close for now till next time.

Your Bro,
Russ

P.S. Oh yes, I think our tour of duty here is 25 missions, but I'm not sure.

Brigadier General James H. Davies

(af.mil)

1945 Brigadier General James H Davies was Commanding General of the 313th Bombardment Wing, located at North Field, Tinian, Mariana Islands. The 509th Composite Group fell within his command. Beyond his normal Wing Command duties when crew member awards were in order it was General Davies who presented the awards in most circumstance. This was true for the other Bombardment Groups under his command consisting of 6th Bombardment Group, 9th Bombardment Group, 504th Bombardment Group, and 505th Bombardment Group.

(af.mil)

Sgt. John R. Kerr 35294052
5th Squad 9th Bomb. Grp
A.P.O. 247 c/o Postmaster
San Francisco, Calif.

1945 Easter Greetings from the Marianas.

John R. Kerr 35294052
5th Squad 9th Bomb. Grp
A.P.O. 247c/o Postmaster
San Francisco, Calif.
May 3, 1945
Thursday, 10 P.M.

Dear Bob & Family,

Well folks right now I am drinking an ice cold bottle of beer on this
nice hot day here in the Marianas. Am sending some picture of me
with my shooting iron. It looked like there not feeding me enough,
but I guess I'm a little trimmer than I used to be. We used to live in
those tents, but now we are in barracks. I have some more pictures
coming yet from Hawaii where we have them developed and
censored. Notice the white coral rock for walks. This makes beautiful
paved roads.

By the way, if you all can buy the "Brief" magazine in your town,
they have a good article in there about the B-29s in the April Edition.
Arnita writes that she intends to come up when she finishes her
house cleaning. Detroit seems to be holding their own in baseball so
far. Are you going to play any tennis this summer, Bob? Well, I guess
that's all I know for the present so keep you flaps down and your tail
up and write.

Your Bro,
Russ

Brief

(wartimepress.com)

5th Squad 9th Bomb. Grp
A.P.O. 247 c/o Postmaster
San Francisco, Calif.
May 7, 1945
Monday 3:30 P.M.

Dear Bro. & Family,

Received your letter today and glad to hear from you. Today is rather warm here and recent showers has moistened things up a little. I've been playing checkers and gin rummy with some of the boys. You had better practice up on your checker playing, Bob, as I'm getting to be quite a checker player (ha). Oh yes, about those pocket books. I've heard a lot about this book "Forever Amber." I wondered if you had that one Bernice.

Today is Sally's big day and I hope she gets along okay. Ronda sure would get a kick out of watching Sally dance as she would have to imitate her. She sure learns fast especially if she thinks anything funny. I suppose your garden is really growing by now. Our pineapples sure are growing. We have to watch our goat from eating the leaves off.

Well, Bob, we finished our 13th mission lately so you can chalk that one up too (ha). Mom said she wasn't feeling so good lately. Arnita wrote that she was coming to see you folks soon. I'll close for now till next time.

Your Bro,
Russ

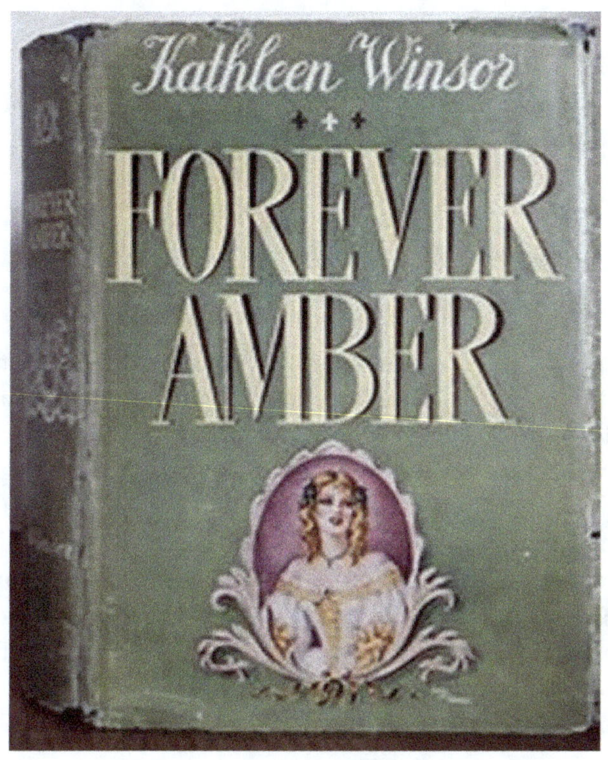

Forever Amber

(abebooks.com)

Sgt. John R. Kerr 35294052
5th Squad 9th Bomb. Grp
A.P.O. 247 c/o Postmaster
San Francisco, Calif.
May 10, 1945
Thur. 12 Noon

Dear Bob & Family,

Well, here comes another letter at you. Thought I would write while I had a little time. The weather here is still rather warm, but a nice breeze is blowing today. I saw a pretty good U.S.O. show last nite staring Gertrude Lawrence. Played some more checkers this morning with our tail gunner then went to a lecture. Our crew got in a confab this morning on how to milk a cow (ha). I said I always milked the first 2 tits facing me (ha). Our tail gunner said he always started by milking the left outer hind one and the right inner front one (ha). So our engineer said he started by milking the 2 hind ones first (ha). We also discussed how to start calves drinking out of a bucket. You should be here to listen in on some of our discussions (ha).

Well we completed our 14th mission the other day. We landed in Iwo Jima on our return to pick up some more fuel. We had to bomb by radar as the target was under an overcast. This was our 2nd mission in Umbriago II. I'll close for now and hope you all are feeling okay.

Your Bro.,
Russ.

Gertrude Lawrence

(discogs.com)

Sgt. John R. Kerr 35294052
5th Squad 9th Bomb. Grp
A.P.O. 247 c/o Postmaster
San Francisco, Calif.
May 13, 1945
Sunday, 1:30 P.M.

Dear Bro & Family,

I suppose you are wondering why I am writing as often. Since you said you were keeping track of my missions I thought I had better report again (ha). We now have 15 missions in. On our last mission we had to bomb the target by radar as it was very soupy weather up there. In fact we ran into a snow storm. On the way back we lost an engine and had to feather it, but we made it to Iwo. It was raining cats and dogs there and we had a heck of a time finding the field. The runway was slippery and we came in with all wheels sliding down the runway (ha), but we finally got stopped. We stayed at Iwo over night and then came back to our base the next day with another crew from our group that had landed for fuel. They still have a few Japs at Iwo that come out in the night, so I slept with one eye open (ha).

The mail room is closed today so I didn't get any mail. I received a letter from Arnita yesterday and she sent me a picture of her and Ronda. Ronda certainly has grown and Arnita is looking good too. I sure am proud of that picture. I went to Church this morning for Mother's Day Services then I wrote to the folks and sent our church program to mom. Oh yes, I ate 4 fried eggs this morning for a breakfast (ha). This afternoon our group played a softball game, but lost 3 -2. They also have a baseball game this evening, which I want to see. Today is a rather nice day here as it is cooler and cloudy. Today is also Henry's birthday.

Well folks guess that's all I know at present and I hope you all are feeling okay. I'll sign off now, so write.

Your Bro,
Russ

P.S. Tell about B-29 being over head.

Sgt. John R. Kerr 35294052
5th Squad 9th Bomb. Grp
A.P.O. 247 c/o Postmaster
San Francisco, Calif.
May 16, 1945
Wednesday, 8:30 P.M.

Dear Bob & Family,

I received your last letter just after I sent you one, so decided to wait a couple of days before I answered it as I answer several letters every day. You folks must feel rather proud of Sally by now. That sure was a swell picture of her in that clipping. In fact you have 2 young ladies to be proud of and I only hope that we can rear Ronda to be as nice as Sally & Georganna.

Well, Bob, I haven't been doing much since I last wrote, but play checkers, eat, and sleep (ha). I think Japan is soon going to have the full capacity of the Allied Air Forces come in on her and our target will be just to hit the Island if its still there. I suppose by now that Arnita has been to see you by now. I made a mistake about those 25 missions. I guess we have to put in more than that, but I don't know exactly how many. I'll sign off for now till next time.

Your Bro.
Russ

Sgt. John R. Kerr 35294052
5th Squad 9th Bomb. Grp
A.P.O. 247 c/o Postmaster
San Francisco, Calif.
May 25, 1945
Friday, 9 A.M.

Dear Bob & Family,

I'm rather ashamed of myself for not writing since last week, but I've been rather busy again lately and I just neglected writing. During this time I have received 2 letters from you folks. Bob's was dated May 12th and Georganna's May 17th. Georganna was telling me how friendly Ronda was to everybody. Didn't I tell you Ronda would try to imitate Sally (ha). I'll bet you folks wore that film of me out showing it to Ronda (ha). Anyway I'm sure Ronda had a nice time and she will probably be pestering her mother to go back to Uncle Bob's real soon. Arnita said they all had a nice time and really enjoyed their trip. That sounds like a good deal, Bob, making another tennis court after the war. Yesterday I had some good old fashion exercises for the first time since I have been here with a pick and shovel (ha). We are building a skeet range for trap shooting and our crew worked on it for about 3 hrs. yesterday forenoon.

Last nite another U.S.O. show invaded the 9th Bomb Grp and it sure was a swell show. It was the play "The Man Who Came to Dinner." Moss Hart wrote this and he played the leading role. He also wrote "The Lady in the Dark", "Winged Victory" and many others. After the show everyone applauded so long that Moss Hart introduced each actor.

Now you will probably want to know something about our missions. The weather hasn't been too good and we have had to ride out several storms of which we have been struck by lightning twice. It really throws a scare into you but it doesn't do any damage. To me it sounded like our bombs had broke loose and fell through the bomb bay doors (ha). Once after the lightning struck I saw a streak of it leave our left wing tip about 20 ft. long (Ha). But on our last mission the weather was perfect and over the Empire we were between 2 layers of clouds. Sometimes the moon really shines bright and you can see as good as daylight. The intelligence dept. sure know their stuff on briefing our course. Read the news about those 29s that raided Tokyo the other day. They practically burned it all down I guess. Boy, they can't burn em all down too soon to suit me. Oh yes, we now have 17 missions in which you are probably interested to know (ha).

Today is a nice cool day here in the Marianas for a change. Arnita writes that it has been rainy and damp back in Ohio.

Say, Bob, that housecleaning during your vacation will really get you back in shape and give you that much needed exercise – won't it Bernice? (Ha) Arnita says that Henry's sure fixed their place up nice.

I am now having classes on electrical work which will probably call for a higher rating.

Well folks guess that's bout all I know at present and I hope you all are feeling okay. I'll try to write more often so don't work too hard and keep em flying,

Your Bro,
Russ

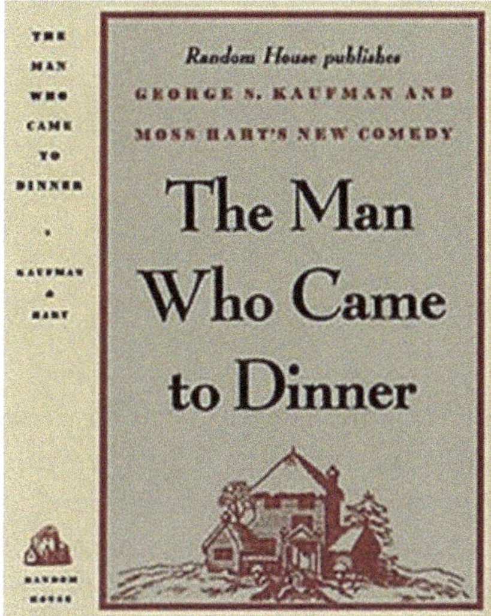

(Random House)

Moss Hart
(theatre.arizona.edu)

Sgt. John R. Kerr 35294052
5th Squad 9th Bomb. Grp
A.P.O. 247 c/o Postmaster
San Francisco, Calif.
Mar 27, 1945
Sunday 3 P.M.

Dear Bob & Family,

Hello everybody, here I am again not knowing exactly what to write about, but you say, Bob, - I'll think of something. It's a little warm today again and I suppose by now your weather is warmer. Been taking it easy this afternoon and should have got some sleep, but it's a little warm for that. Recently we finished our 18th mission, which wasn't a bad mission. Everything worked okay and we saw no flak nor fighters, although we were over the Empire for over an hour. It was a nice moonlight night and clear over our target. Those boys sure did a good job in Tokyo the other night of which you have probably heard. Well tomorrow we have the day off and I hope I get some mail as it has been several days since I have received any. Hope you all are okay and I'll close now till next time.

Your Bro.
Russ

Sgt. John R. Kerr 35294052
5th Squad 9th Bomb. Grp
A.P.O. 247 c/o Postmaster
San Francisco, Calif.
May 30, 1945
Wednesday, 8:30 P.M.

Dear Bob & Family.

Boy-o-boy I sure have been getting the letters here lately. I think I got 10 in the last two days. Today I received 2 from you and 2 from Mom & Dad and two from Arnita. Well as you say, Bob, all I've got to write is the same old shit story (ha). Sure am glad that you all write so often. Whenever you see a guy down in the dumps around here you can bet he hasn't been receiving any letters from home. Well, Bob, since our 18th mission we have been sort of resting up and one gets sort of restless just resting if you get what I mean. Say where did you all get that pretty green ink your using?

You was talking about Detroit's baseball team. Well the boys over here watch the baseball scores with much interest and they post the scores in our bulletin board everyday. Why don't you all get rid of that Rudy York – he's getting too old to play ball anyway (ha). Your probably right about me not being able to hit a Jap with that revolver because I've never fired it as yet and hope I don't have to. It's really not for that purpose but it would come in handy if I met up with one. Played a little hard ball this evening with the boys then took a shower and started writing letters. Didn't go to the show tonite as it was some G.I. shorts. Saw some good movies though this week – one was "Practically Yours" and another was "Bring on the Girls"

Mom wrote and said she wished that we would start to give Ronda darning lessons, but she is a little too young at present, don't you folks think so? Arnita says Ronda has been out the last couple of days and got a little sun burned. She also said that Ronda heard and saw it hailing in the window and she said "Look mommy its raining peanuts."

Mom said that Dad sure has a time getting his chewing tobacco. She has to stand in line there at Lima for 6 hours and then sometimes there out by that time. Sure glad I can get cigarettes over here.

Well tomorrow is pay day and then the 1st of June we can start getting our allotment of beer again. Over here in this climate a bottle of beer goes a long way toward making you Island happy (ha). I could probably drink you under the table nowadays Bob – well part way anyway.

Say, Bernice, how is your Dad by now? I don't believe Bob mentioned it in his letter. I'll bet the girls will be tickled when there vacation comes around. I'm sure they will want to spend some time with Arnita & Ronda.

We haven't had any of those round table discussions about the farm lately, but the other night we had quite a discussion about horses that had the heaves (ha).

Well folks, guess that's bout all I know for the present. Hope you all are okay and feeling good. I suppose, Bob you will be back to the job by the time you receive this with a nice sun tan and all pepped up. I'll end this rigamarole now and write to Arnita and Ronda, so keep em flying.

As Ever Your Bro.
Russ

P.S. I'll take you on in a checker game anytime anywhere (ha).

Rudy York
(4.opblogsport.com)

Practically Yours
(Amazon.com)

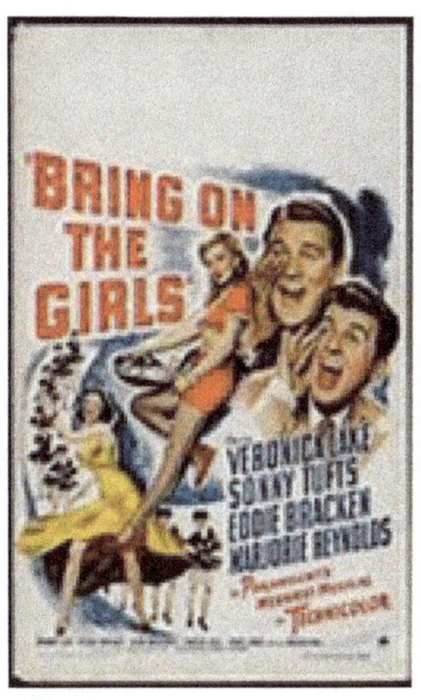

Bring on the Girls
(movieposters.ha.com)

Sgt. John R. Kerr 35294052
5th Squad 9th Bomb. Grp
A.P.O. 247 c/o Postmaster
San Francisco, Calif.
June 2, 1945
Saturday, 6:30 P.M.

Dear Bob & Family,

Thought I would drop you another line or two as we now have completed 19 missions okay. I suppose your all done with your housecleaning by now. I received a V-Mail letter from Strands and they seem to be getting along okay. Say the PX hasn't any beer in as yet, but I hope they do have soon. I can't tell you much about this last mission, Bob, but I'll bet you sure would be surprised at things I have already seen. Well I want to go to the show tonight as I missed it last night. Played some cards today to pass away a little time. Guess that's bout all I know at present so I'll sign off for now till next time.

Your Bro,
Russ

Sgt. John R. Kerr 35294052
5th Squad 9th Bomb. Grp
A.P.O. 247 c/o Postmaster
San Francisco, Calif.
June 6, 1945
Wednesday, 2 P.M.

Dear Bob & Family,

It's rather warm and sultry here today and it behooves me to think of much to write, but I'll do my best. As I said before, I would keep you informed of our missions, so now we have in 20. We had a little rough weather on the way up, but it was clear over Japan. Saw lots of flak over the target area and rather accurate. We also had a mess of fighters to put up with and they were very aggressive. They really acted like they were mad. Anyway the 9th Bomb Grp. Had credit for 16 of them and 2 probables. Our place in the formation was so that our plane had no direct attacks and we could not fire for fear of hitting other B-29s, but we did get in a few bursts. Our bomb bay doors wouldn't close after the bomb run and we had to close them by hand about 2 hours later. We made nice time on the trip which only took 14 hrs. Well so much for that. Oh yes, I did see a Jap plane ram the rudder of a B-29 and knocked it off, but the B-29 made it back and the Jap hit the silk.

I received your letter yesterday and I was wondering, Bob, if you were a member of this Melvindale Junior Chamber of Commerce? Maybe some day you will be a big business executive or something.

The folks wrote that those peas were 4 in. high now, so I'll have something to tell the boys now. Arnita sent a clipping out of the paper of a boy I used to run around with. He had been liberated from a German prison camp. He was a gunner on a B-17.

Well folks, that's bout all I know for the present so I'll close.

Your Bro.

Russ

P.S. Please don't mention to Arnita bout our missions as I would rather have it that way. Thanks.

B-17 Flying Fortress Bomb Bay Doors Open

(2michaejlt)

Sgt. John R. Kerr 35294052
5th Squad 9th Bomb. Grp
A.P.O. 247 c/o Postmaster
San Francisco, Calif.
June 9, 1945
Sat. 9:30 A.M.

Dear Bob & Family,

I have 2 letters here in front of me from you folks dated May 26 &
May 30 and will attempt to answer them today. Sure glad to hear
from you all so often. We have had several showers today and the
weather is much cooler. The folks say that those peas are now in
bloom and next month will be ready to hull. Been sort of resting up
today not doing anything but play cards. I started this letter at 9:30
this morn, but it is now about 4 P.M. I just received another letter
from Arnita and she says Ronda bout runs her little legs off playing
outdoors.

Well Bob recently we put in our 21st mission although we saw no
enemy fighters and very little flak. The weather was an overcast over
the target and cold not see the results. On our return we landed at
Iwo for fuel and stayed overnite. We left the next day about noon.
They sure treat a person nice there. They gave us cigarettes, beer,
gum, which is more than we have been getting here lately. Our beer
here is due anytime now.

I went to the P.X. today and got some cigarettes, gum, candy, towel
and a box of crackers, which they just got in.

I guess that's bout all I know for today, so don't you all work too
hard and keep em flying.

Your Bro,
Russ

Sgt. John R. Kerr 35294052
5th Squad 9th Bomb. Grp
A.P.O. 247 c/o Postmaster
San Francisco, Calif.
Tinian Island
June 15, 1945
Friday 7:30 P.M.

Dear Bob & Family,

Received your letter dated June 5 yesterday and I just found time to write this evening. Although I am a little tired, I shaved, took a shower, and came down here to the G. F. Dive to write this letter. Our club is down here by the theatre among lots of little fir trees and it sure is a swell place. They have ping pong tables, pool tables, sell cokes and ice cream, and a nice place to write letters. It's something like a service club back in the States. Yes, Bob, I also saw the picture of the new Ford in one of our papers and they sure are nice looking. Say those Tigers are bucking for first place in the league aren't they?

I received a letter from Arnita yesterday and she said Ronda likes to ride the neighbors kids tricycle and she sure knows how to ride it (ha).

The weather here has been rather nice lately with showers every once in a while and not too hot.

Well, Bob we now have in 22 missions and in our last one we came clear back from Japan on 3 engines. We lost all our oil from one and had to feather it. Anyway the weather was soupy and thick up there and we got tossed around quite a bit.

Guess I'll go to the shore now and then I'll have to write Arnita her letter, so don't work too hard and I'll write later.

Your Bro.
Russ

Sgt. John R. Kerr 35294052
398th Sqd 504th Bomb Grp.
A.P.O. 247 c/o Postmaster
San Francisco, Calif.
Tinian Island
June 19, 1945
Tuesday, 9 A.M.

Dear Bob & Family,

Thought I had better drop you a few lines to let you know that I now have a new address. We have moved to a different Bomb Grp and Sqd. otherwise my address is the same. Its 398th Sqd. 504th Bomb Grp. I still go to the 9th and pick up my mail everyday as it is only ½ mi down the road. We will probably start flying again soon. Saw a good stage show here last nite with about 6 gals in the cast. I suppose, Bob, that you have got everything straightened out at your job by now. Lyman wrote that his place was now for sale, but he said they want too much for it. Well that's all I know for the present, but I'll write later. I now have a meeting to attend. So don't work too hard and I'll write later.

Your Bro.
Russ

Sgt. John R. Kerr 35294052
398th Sqd 504th Bomb Grp.
A.P.O. 247c/o Postmaster
San Francisco, Calif.
Tinian Island
June 27, 1945
Wednesday 8:00 A.M.

Dear Bob & Family,

When I wrote my last letter, I also wrote it in the morning and at the time I said I was expecting a letter from you folks – well I did that afternoon. It was dated June 13th. Say, Grandad sure gets around for his age doesn't he? Decoration day. Arnita took him out to the cemetery and he told her about each one that was buried there. He generally hops on a bus and goes right to our house then Arnita usually takes him back. If he is there when you get this, tell him hello for me. Sorry to hear that Geo. Emlich has been sick for so long and I hope he gets better soon. You can tell him that from me. I imagine your weather is warmer by now so that your peas will probably be big peas some day (ha). Well, Bob, yesterday was my birthday and what a celebration I had. Recently we went on our 24th mission. They have assigned us to a brand new B-29 and this was its first mission. The target was sacked in by weather so we went over the target by ourselves. I guess the only danger was trying to miss other B-29s in the soup. Anyway we had no trouble and returned here to our base okay. Saw a good show last nite called "Brewsters Millions". Its a fairly good show. I haven't had any letters for 3 days now and I hope today that I get forty eleven. I guess that's bout all I know at present so I'll close for now.

Your Bro.
Russ

P.S. This is onion skin paper I borrowed off another member of the crew. Large isn't it?

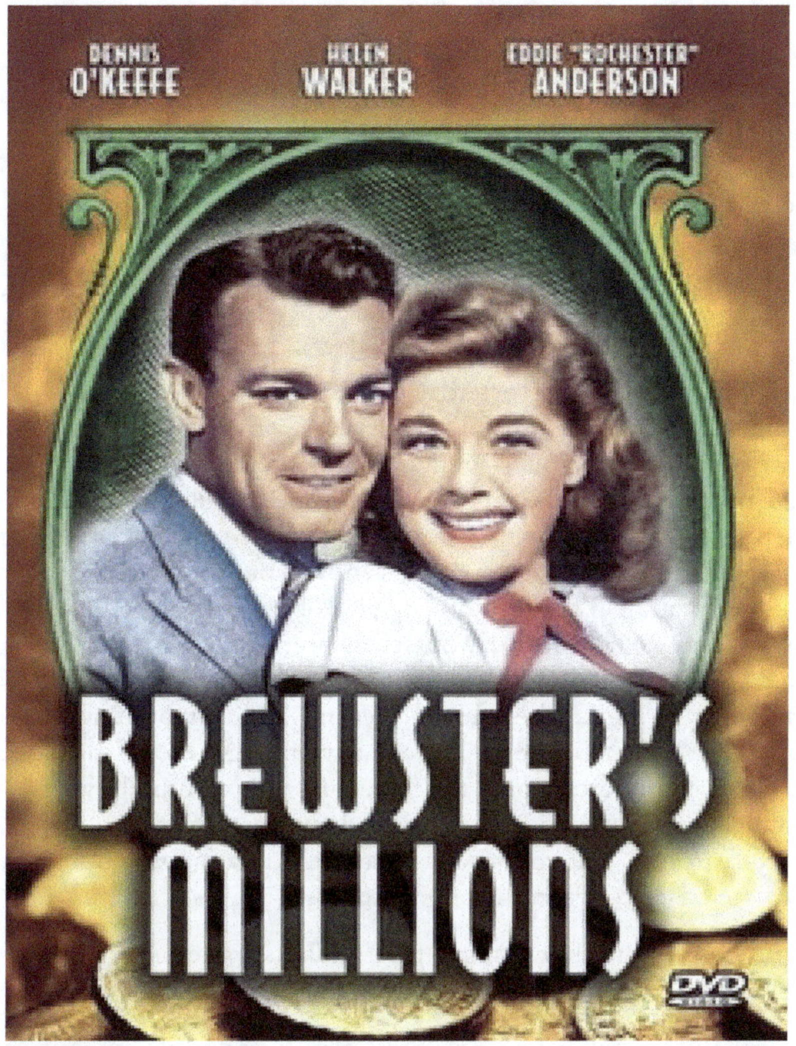

Brewster's Millions

(dvdempire.com)

Sgt. John R. Kerr 35294052
398th Sqd 504th Bomb Grp.
A.P.O. 247c/o Postmaster
San Francisco, Calif.
Tinian Island
June 29, 1945
Friday, 5 P.M.

Dear Bob & Family,

Received your last letter yesterday dated June 18th, but am just finding time to answer. I received 3 letters from Arnita today and her report is the same as yours – rain and more rain. Glad to hear that Dad Emlich is getting better now and I hope he will be able to be back on his feet soon. I sure was surprised to see Detroit on top of the league and I imagine everybody is now wondering if Hank Greenberg can help them or not. Well, Bob, we now have in 25 missions and we can consider ourselves pretty lucky I guess. I write Arnita the number of missions I put in, but I never tell her of the details which I think is best not to. Recently we flew our 2nd mission in our new ship and our 3rd since we have been in the 504th B. Grp. There was an undercast over the target and also clouds above us, so we didn't see much only a little flak and automatic fire with tracers from the ground. The moon was shining through bright enough for me to see other B-29s in the target area.

I want to go to the show tonite and I think its something about Blondie.

I understand we will have a 4 day rest here starting July 2nd and the tail gunner and I are going to Guam. We also will have a Jeep to drive during this time. I'll close for now and tell Granddad to catch one for me and I'll drop one for him.

Your Bro,
Russ

Hank Greenberg

(ebay.com)

Sgt. John R. Kerr 35294052
398th Sqd 504th Bomb Grp.
A.P.O. 247c/o Postmaster
San Francisco, Calif.
Tinian Island
July 2, 1945
Monday 5 P.M.

Dear Bro & Family,

Well, Bob, it sure is a hot day here on good old Tinian Island and I
hope it rains to cool things off. I imagine that you folks are wishing
for sunshine. I went down to the 9th this morning and I had one
letter from you folks and that was all. It was dated June 23. Then I
tried to sleep and rest up a little but I guess it was too warm. I also
bought some film today so I'll be taking some more pictures. Say,
Bob, I didn't think you was due for that Old Timers League, but I
don't know maybe I'm ready for that league also (ha). I see that
Detroit is still hanging on to the lead by a small margin. Yes, Bob, I'll
bet them Japs are really mad by now, in fact I'll bet they're really
burning up.

Well, recently we completed our 26th mission and we had good flying
weather. It was clear over the target, but light enough to read a
newspaper in our plane. We had a little flak and a hail of tracers from
automatic weapons coming our way. That new plane of ours sure
does churn up good and as yet we haven't a hole in it. Of course we
all had the usual dose of medicine after we got back (ha). Guess thats
all for now except tomorrow we start a 4 day leave from all duties
along with a Jeep to ride in.

Your Bro.
Russ

Sgt. John R. Kerr 35294052
398th Sqd 504th Bomb Grp.
A.P.O. 247c/o Postmaster
San Francisco, Calif.
Tinian Island
July 14, 1945
Saturday 7:30 A.M.

Dear Bob & Family,

It's a little early in the morning, but I just ate chow and feel pretty good, except for a few sore muscles developed while pitching all yesterday. I received your letter yesterday which by the way was addressed to the 9th Bomb Grp and as I was a little tired, I decided I would think of more to write this morning after a good nites rest, but now I find out that I'll need to rub down or something (Ha) Guess I'll have to join the old timers league. Your letter was dated July 3rd and one of the boys brought it over here the same day it came. Say, how do you like V-mail letters. Can you read them very good? They really make them small. I'll bet you all had a good time fishing in Canada. Glad to hear your garden is doing better. That 500 batting average, Bob sounds pretty good, but I'll bet you can place the darn ball most anywhere you want to with that easy pitching. We dug up a team from the combat section on the spur of the moment yesterday to play another Sqd. I pitched, our radio operator played 1st and our tail gunner played right field and our co-pilot played 3rd base so you see our crew was pretty well represented. We had a good infield, but every time they hit one to the outfield our fielders would make an error. Anyway we got beat 6 – 2. They only had 4 hits and I think we had about 5 hits.

I don't know whether I told you this before or not, but our officers are all 1st Lts. now except our A. C. and he is now a Captain. Sure was glad to see them get promoted. Arnita says that Ronda still takes a notion to do acrobatics now and then. Henry is always on hand when they need a man's help around the house and on the car. Henry, Arnita and Ronda all went to the circus the other nite and it rained them out. I guess Ronda sure enjoyed herself.

It is now raining cats & dogs, which isn't very unusual here lately. I saw a good show last nite called "Cinderella Jones". Well, Bob, recently we finished our 28th mission and the only thing rough about it was the weather I guess. There was an undercast over the target. We had all our lights on and you could see other planes with their lights on everywhere. We now have over 400 combat flying hrs. in which isn't hay exactly. We have about 3 Oak Leaf Clusters to be added to our Air Medal and the D.T.C. coming up. But I don't care about that as long as we finish our tour of duty okay. 7 more to go, so keep your fingers crossed.

Your Bro.
Russ

Cinderella Jones
(Remick Music Company)

3 Oak Leaf Clusters
(medalsofamerica.com)

Sgt. John R. Kerr 35294052
398th Sqd 504th Bomb Grp.
A.P.O. 247c/o Postmaster
San Francisco, Calif.
Tinian Island
July 10, 1945
Tuesday 7 P.M.

Dear Bob & Family,

It is now raining a steady rain here and I got a little wet at the show. Although it was a good show "Circumstantial Evidence", I haven't heard from you all for quite some time. Our 4 day rest leave stretched out to be about 7 days, but now we are back on the balls again and hope to finish our missions up within a month. I'm rather positive that we will have to pull 35 missions. Recently we finished our 27th mission okay. Yesterday I received 2 letters from Arnita and one from the folks. This was the first I had received in 3 days. I received the Lima News also which only took 10 days to get there and today I received a later edition that took a little longer. Oh yes, our airplane commander was made Captain today.

Well, Bob, I suppose your garden is coming out of it now. Sure could go for some of that Detroit Beer (ha). When I get back we will have to celebrate if you can take it (ha). Well, I'll close for now until next time and don't work too hard.

Your Bro.
Russ

Circumstantial Evidence

(alchetron.com)

Sgt. John R. Kerr 35294052
398th Sqd 504th Bomb Grp.
A.P.O. 247c/o Postmaster
San Francisco, Calif.
Tinian Island
July 18, 1945
Wed. 9 A.M.

Dear Bob & Family,

Received your last letter day before yesterday and am just finding time to answer it. My mail has been coming through good here lately. Well I might as well start out with a little gossip from home as thats what everybody writes me and I'll just pass it on (ha). Virginia Collins husband has applied for a divorce. He is now home from Europe on furlough. Lenore has applied for a divorce from Virgil and Jr. is in the S.W. Pacific on a torpedo boat.

Arnita writes that she has been having tire trouble. One day she ran a wire in a tire and the next day it was a roofing nail in another tire. Henry's and Arnita and Ronda went to the circus the other night and Henry's car caught on fire from a short in the horn (ha). More trouble. I saw a good show last nite "A Tree Grows in Brooklyn". It was a little sad, but a good picture. I guess Dad has been busy hulling peas.

Yesterday I slept all afternoon as we just got back from our 29th mission around 9:30 A.M. We took off the night before about 7P.M. to drop some fire bombs on Kuana [Kuwana] – a little town near Nagoya. We couldn't see the town as there was a thick cloud coverage, but there sure was a big red glow. One big cloud of smoke went up to about 20,000 ft. We went through one of these smoke clouds once and it shook us up and down. In fact my head was hitting the top of the plane more than my setter was hitting the seat (ha).

We have another ball game this afternoon and I'm now over my soreness from the last one we played. Say Detroit sure is going to town aren't they? They have been in the lead now for quite some time. I'm sorry to hear that Dad Emlich had to go back to the hospital. Tell him I send my best wishes for his recovery.

The weather around here has been rather rainy. I guess its now that time of the year for them here in Tinian. Arnita writes that Ronda is sure getting a tan from being outdoors most of the time. They were out home the other nite and her and Dad had quite a time playing. I suppose when I get back that I'll be quite busy entertaining her.

I'll close for now, so take it easy and tell the girls I said "hello".

Your Bro,
Russ

A Tree Grows in Brooklyn

(subscene.com)

Sgt. John R. Kerr 35294052
398th Sqd 504th Bomb Grp.
A.P.O. 247c/o Postmaster
San Francisco, Calif.
Tinian Island
July 20th, 1945
Thur. 7 P.M.

Dear Bob & Family,

Hello everybody. Well I just finished chow and I feel pretty good. We just got back from a mission this morning so I ate breakfast (eggs) and hit the sack. I didn't get up until 5 P.M. this evening. We took off about 7:30 last nite and we had pretty good flying weather. We hit a small town about 80 mi. from Toykyo called Choshi. I guess we were over land only about 20 sec. We have been over Japan for 2 hrs on missions before so I guess this was the shortest period over the Mainland. It was a solid undercast until we was over the target and I guess the heat from the fires broke open the clouds. One boy was flying over the top of us on the bomb run and he sure got a good cussing from us only he couldn't hear us (Ha). Anyway we had our lights on, so he went to the left of us. We haven't fired our guns for the last 10 missions and I hope we don't have to on our next 5 as that is all we have left now. We now have 30 missions in. Well it is now time for the show "The Corn is Green", so I'll sign off for now until later. I still have to write Arnita yet tonite and also Lyman.

Your Bro,
Russ
Picture enclosed

John Russell (Russ) Kerr, Tinian Island, July 1945

The Corn is Green

(filmous.com)

Sgt. John R. Kerr 35294052
398th Sqd 504th Bomb Grp.
A.P.O. 247c/o Postmaster
San Francisco, Calif.
Tinian Island
July 26, 1945
Thur. 1 P.M.

Dear Bob & Family,

I received Georganna's letter about 3 days ago and during that time I
am just finding time to write as we pulled 2 missions over the empire
within 3 days. We just got back from our 32nd mission this morning.
Our 31st mission (day before yesterday) we hit Nagoya with
demolition bombs about noon and about the same time the Navy
was striking also. That day there was over 2,000 planes over Japan at
the same time and boy was that a sight. Last nite we layed mines on
the other side of Japan. We went clear across Japan and then back
again. It sure was a moonlight nite but there was an undercast under
us. The weather was a little rough though. When we go through
those thunder heads it sure tosses us around. The rest of the boys are
all sleeping now so guess I had better get some sleep too. I'm a little
tired, but glad that we only have 3 more missions to pull. We might
finish by the 1st of August.

Your Bro,
Russ

Tinian Island, July 29, '45, Sun. morn. 8 A.M.

Dear Bob and family,

Well, here it is, Sun. morning, rather early, but I guess this is my only time to write as we sure have been busy lately and we are taking off again this forenoon. We finished our 33rd mission yesterday and I can consider ourselves a rather lucky crew. The weather was rough all the way up there, but when we got over Japan it was clear as a crystal and the moon was shining bright. We was going along just fine on our mine run, but just before mines away about 12 search lights bracketed us from all sides and we couldn't see anything from the glare of those lights. Anyway the pilot put our plane in a dive and some evasive action for speed and the flak was bursting where we were before that. When we got out of there I saw another plane catching what we had just went through and then I wondered how we actually got through ourselves. Anyway we only had one hole in the tail and it was a small one. So far we have been hit three times in our missions. It looks like we will finish by the first of this (Aug) month- just two more to go. I think today we go to China or along the China Coast. I saw Eddie Bracken and his show here last nite. Well guess I'll have to go now. Oh yes, by the time you receive this letter, you won't have to write me here anymore.

Your bro,
Russ.

Eddie Bracken
(ww2online.org)

Sgt. John R. Kerr 35294052
398th Sqd 504th Bomb Grp.
A.P.O. 247c/o Postmaster
San Francisco, Calif.
Tinian Island
July 30, 1945
Monday 6:30 P.M.

Dear Bob & Family,

Received your letter today dated July 20. It seems like 10 days is what it takes for our letters on a one way trip. I've been in the sack practically all day today as I didn't have any sleep last nite . We took off yesterday at 11:30 A.M. for Iwo to refuel and make one of those long missions along the coast of Manchuria. On the way to Iwo, one of our engines was acting up and a few other things were wrong. We landed there with a full load of mines and boy I sure sweat that landing. We ate chow there and filled our tanks with gas and oil. So we took off from there about 7:30 P.M. with just enough power to get off the ground. Our engine was still acting up, so we decided to mine in Japan (a secondary field). We then came back to base and landed about 5:30 A.M. Later we found out that #1 engine had 6 dead cylinders. So they are now putting on a new engine. We will get credit for a mission and I'm glad we didn't have to abort as that was our 34th mission – one more to go, which I hope to finish tomorrow, which will be a dumb mission. We will carry no mines but act as rescue ship for other B 29s.

Yes, I received G. Lou's letter and say, Bob, about that 30 -0 score of that ball game. Was that in a ball park or on a race track? (Ha) That half barrel of beer sounds good especially in warm weather.

Glad to hear that Dad Emlich is feeling much better. By the way, Bob, I notice that your letters are getting longer and they read just like you would be talking to me. Thats the kind of letter I like to get, but I guess there is no need for you to write to me here anymore after you receive this letter as by that time I expect to be in the States.

Anyway I hope so although I will still keep you informed of my whereabouts.

I guess I'll go to the show tonite as it is a pretty good show "Royal Scandal". Say that was a pretty good story about that tail gunner.

Don't forget that beer party or anything else (hah).

Your Bro,
Russ

A Royal Scandal
(thesoundofvincentprice.com)

Sgt. John R. Kerr 35294052
398th Sqd 504th Bomb Grp.
A.P.O. 336 c/o Postmaster
San Francisco, Calif.
Tinian Island
Aug. 4, 1945
Saturday, Noon

Dear Bob & Family,

Just received your letter dated July 25 and glad to hear from you. I also received 3 from Arnita and one from the folks. These are the first letters I have received since 2 days ago. Arnita sent me some pictures of her and Ronda and also of Mom & Dad. They are all swell pictures and I can sure see a change in Ronda. Arnita said that the temperature there was up to 101 and that sure is hot. I don't believe the temperature here gets over 90 nor under 70 so that's a happy medium I guess. Anyway she said that it was so warm that she finally ventured out in her shorts (ha). She also said I had some back wages coming from the Westinghouse maybe 50 cents or more she doesn't know. Guess we will have to use that for our second honeymoon (ha). Mom wrote that Dad is busy making hay – 70 acres. I receive on an average about 1 letter a week from them. Sorry to hear that Dad Emlich had to go back to the hospital.

I see in here Detroit is still leading the league by quite a margin and I guess your team isn't doing so bad either. That beer is worth playing for. We have been getting practically all the beer we want here lately. As yet our cigarettes are holding out pretty good. Well, Bob, our pups are growing fast. The dog in our barracks had 7 pups and she sure has a job keeping them pacified. I saw a good movie here last night "Slightly Dangerous."

Well, Bob, we started out in our 35th mission about 3 days ago, but we lost an engine about 1 ½ hrs from base, so we had to come back all P.O.'d. Now we will have to sweat it out again. We have over 500 hours of combat flying time in now. Yesterday was a holiday for everybody and we all just lapped around. Oh yes, there has a been a change in rank for most of our crew. I am now a Staff Sgt. which calls for a little more pay (ha).

Guess that's all I know for sure, so I'll sign off now until next time.

Your Bro.
Russ

Slightly Dangerous
(moviepostershop.com)

S/Sgt John R. Kerr 35294052
398 Sqd. 504 Bomb Grp
A.P.O. #336 c/o P.M.
San Francisco, Calif.
Tinian Island
Aug. 8, 1945
Wednesday, 9P.M.

Dear Bob & Family,

Today was a day of celebration for our crew and we did just that. Much beer was consumed by all as we are now finished with our tour of duty over here and in about another week we will probably be started for the States. I haven't received any letter for 2 days now, but I thought you would like to know this. I'm sure Arnita will be happy and I know I am (Ha).

I saw Enos Slaughter , Max West, Joe Gordon and several other big leagues play ball this afternoon. I'll close for now and let you know of further developments later.

Your bro,
Russ

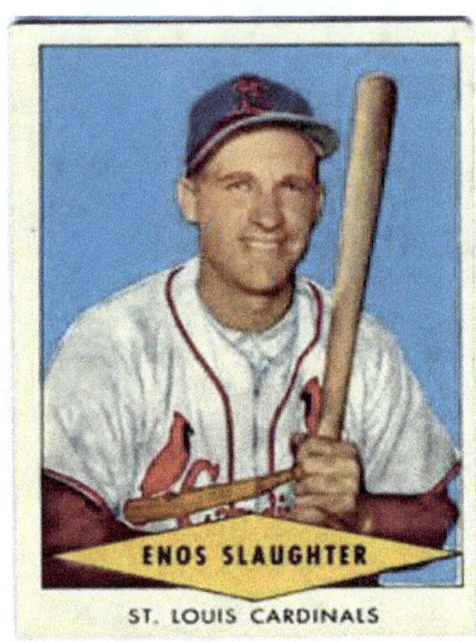

Enos Slaughter
(quotationof.com)

Max West
(vintagecardprices.com)

Joe Gordon
(imageshack.com)

S/Sgt. John R. Kerr 35294052
398th Sqd 504th Bomb Grp.
A.P.O. 336 c/o Postmaster
San Francisco, Calif.
Tinian
Aug. 16, 1945
Thur 6 P.M.

Dear Bob & Family,

Received your last letter day before yesterday and thought by now that I could write I was on my way home, but our orders haven't come through as yet and we are still sweating it out. But I think it will be tomorrow or the next day, I'm sure. We had chicken tonite for chow for a change and it sure was good. All I've been doing lately is to play checkers and wait. I have already turned in the most of my equipment in and I'm practically all ready to go. I don't know as yet whether we go by boat or plane. I'll write the day I leave and let you know.

Your Bro.,
Russ

Non-Commissioned Officers' Club
Herington Army Air Filed
Herington, Kansas
Dec. 7, 1945
10:30 P.M.

Dear Peoples,

Well, here I am now in Kansas, so thought I would drop you a line. I will be here long enough for an answer. I arrived here Dec. 5th and Arnita also started for Kansas City the same day. I talked with her on the telephone this afternoon and she said she and Ronda were a little tired.

I whether I get a pass or not or when she can come here to awhile. This is a swell place with good chow, nice people, and a nice N.C.O. Club. I have my share of the beer I guess (ha).

Did you have a good time Xmas. Tell the girls I think that Santa Claus will be traveling in a B-29 next year.

Ronda sure had a swell time over her Xmas presents. Did you get my B-29 card?

Well it is rather late and about my bedtime now and since our mail [will] be censored from this base, I guess I have to sign off. Hope to hear from you soon,

Your Bro.
Russ.
Mr. Russell Kerr

CLOSE CALL

John R. Kerr, Gunner, 5th Squadron

We were flying at 3000' enroute to Japan on a daylight mission. I was half asleep when I was startled to see trees coming up under our left wing. With a yell to the AC who saw them at the same time, I watched Capt Klemme pull the left wing up with full throttle just narrowly missing those trees. Whew!
We later learned that the volcanic isle was also 3000'.

[9th Bombardment Group (VH) History, p.322.]

MISSIONS

The following is a list of aircrews (by airplane commander's names) and command and staff. At briefings, they were given a primary and secondary target. If for any reason they couldn't bomb either, they were to pick out any other target in their flight path; i.e., a target of opportunity (TO). Robert E. Klemme, AC on the "Umbriago."

February 9th #1 TRUK

These were "warm-up" combat missions that were flown to Truk, a Japanese held island about 700 miles southeast of Tinian and to Iwo Jima. Both of these missions were what we termed "milk runs;" i.e., some anti-aircraft flak over the target, but no great danger. P 19. (9th Bombardment Group (VH) History, p. 19)

The group flew its first mission to Truk on FEB 9th with 30 aircraft. Colonel Eisenhart led that mission. P 145. (9th Bombardment Group (VH) History, p, 145)

February 12th #2 IWO JIMA

One of the major hazards from the beginning of B-29 operations from the Marianas was the prospect of having to ditch at sea on the way back from Japan, in case battle damage or mechanical problems resulted in not being able to make the distance to home base. So, the creation of an emergency base on Iwo Jima was highly important.

Iwo is about 6 miles long and 4 miles wide (See map.) For weeks in February it had been "softened" up by B-29 bombing and by naval ship bombardment (the heaviest shelling of the war) in preparation for the invasion by the Marines on February 19th.

The principal grand strategy purpose of taking Iwo was to provide a base for the VII Fighter Command, the P-51 fighters which were to accompany our daylight missions to mainland off Japan to help take care of Japanese defense fighter aircraft and to perform strafing runs on Japanese ground targets. The planned secondary purpose was to provide an emergency landing base for crippled B-29s returning from missions over Japan. This purpose proved, by far, to be the more important. pp 19-20. (9th Bombardment Group (VH) History p. pp. 19-20.)

February 25th **#5 TOKYO**

March 4th **#6 TOKYO (BOMBED SECONDARY DUE TO FLIGHT CONDITIONS)**

March 11th **#8 NAGOYA URBAN**

March 13th **#9 OSAKA URBAN**

March 16th **#10 KOBE URBAN**

March 27 **#13 MINING**

March 30 **#14 MINING**

April 1st **#15 MINING, KURE APPROACHES**

April 7th **#17 MITSUBISHI A/C, NAGOYA**
Abort-mech

April 13th **#20 TOKYO ARSENSAL**

April 18th **#22 KOKUBU AIRFIELD**

April 26th **#27 MIYAZAKI AIRFIELD**
Failed Take Off

April 27th **#28 KOKUBU AIRFIELD**

April 30th **#30 TACHIKAWA AIR ARSENAL**
Failed Take Off

May 5th & 6th **#32 MINING, TOKYO & ISE BAYS & INLAND SEA.**
Super Dumbo

May 8th **#33 & #34 OITA A/F & MATSUYAMA A/F**

May 11th **#36 & #37 MIYAKONOJO & MIYAZAKI AIRFIELDS**

May 20th	**#41 MINING, MIYAZU & MAIZURU BAYS**
May 22nd	**#42 MINING, SHIMONOSEKI STRAITS**
May 27th	**#44 MINING, FUHIKI, KARATSU, FUKUOKA BAYS**
June 1st	**#46 OSAKA URBAN AREA** Super Dumbo
June 5th	**#47 KOBE URBAN AREA**
June 7th	**#48 OSAKA URBAN AREA**
June 15th	**#50 OSAKA AMAGASAKI URBAN AREA** Bombed Target of Opportunity (9th Bombardment Group…Pp 145-156)

MAPS

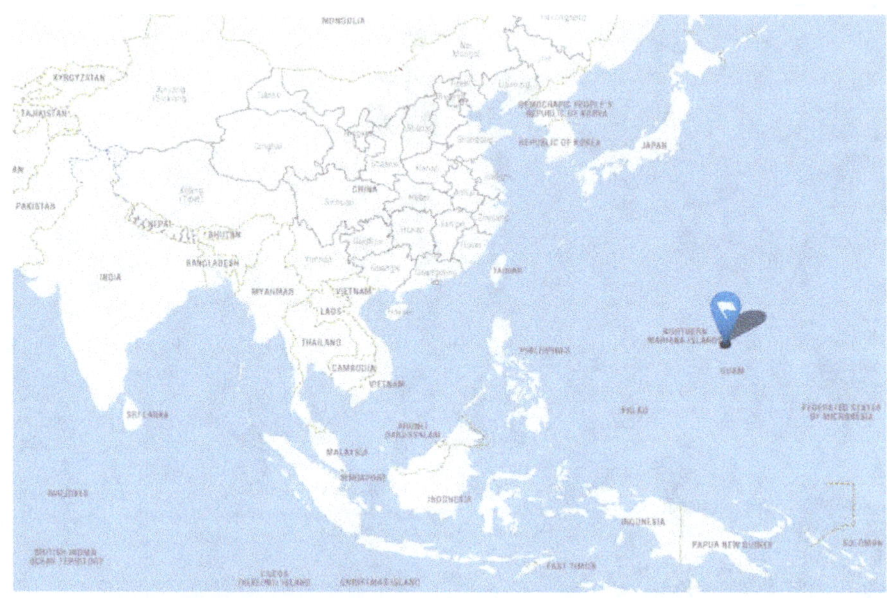

MAP OF NORTHERN MARIANA ISLANDS
Worldmap1com/Northern-Mariana-Islands-map.asp

Tinian Island
ww2online.org

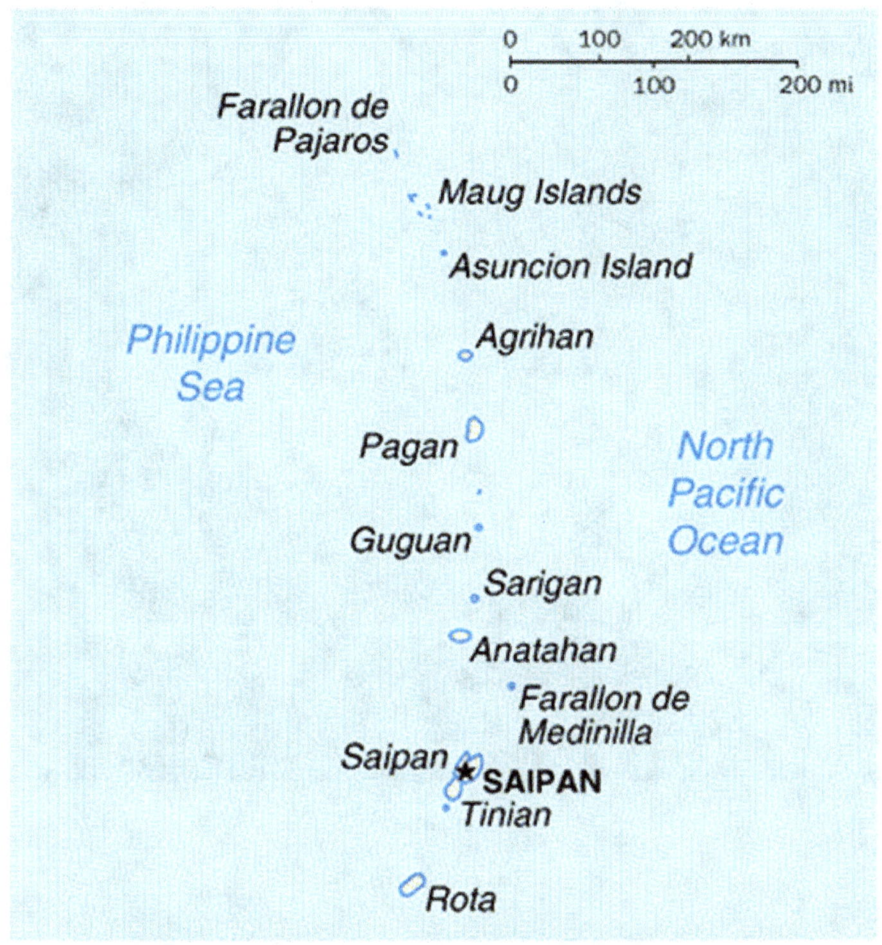

NORTHERN MARIANA ISLANDS LOCATION MAP

Worldmap1com/Northern-Mariana-Islands-map.asp

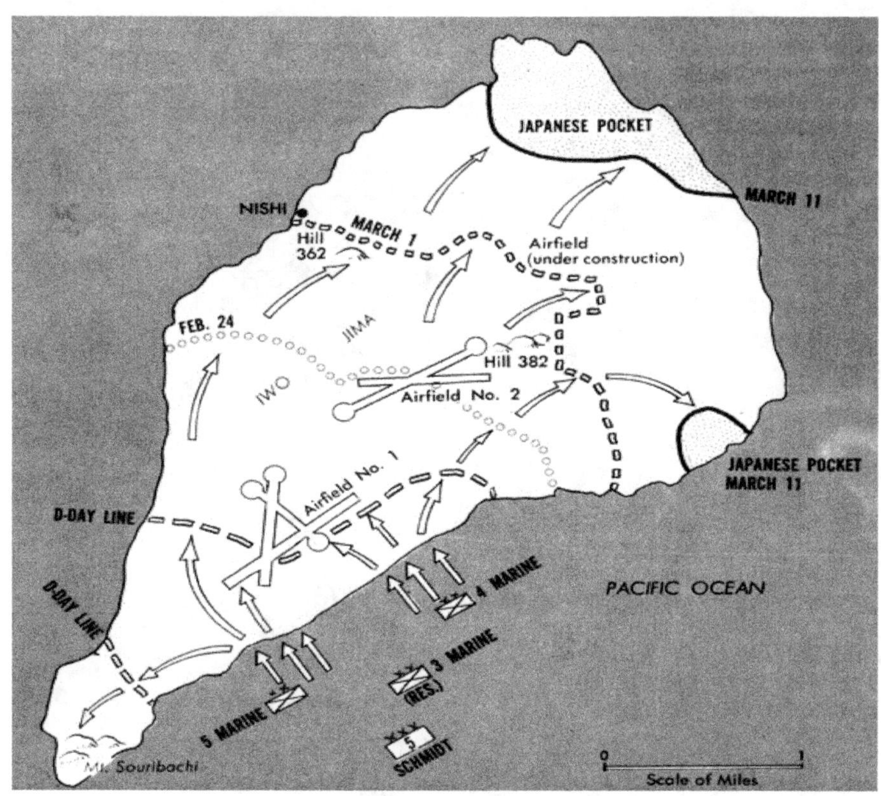

Iwo Jima

(onwar.com)

Tokyo was hit by incendiaries on 25 February 1945 when 174 B-29s flew a high altitude raid during daylight hours and destroyed around 643 acres (260 ha) (2.6 km 2) of the snow-covered city, using 453.7 tons of mostly incendiaries with some fragmentation bombs.

Date: 1945

Location: Tokyo, Japan

Result: American victory

Toyko, Japan

(onwar.com)

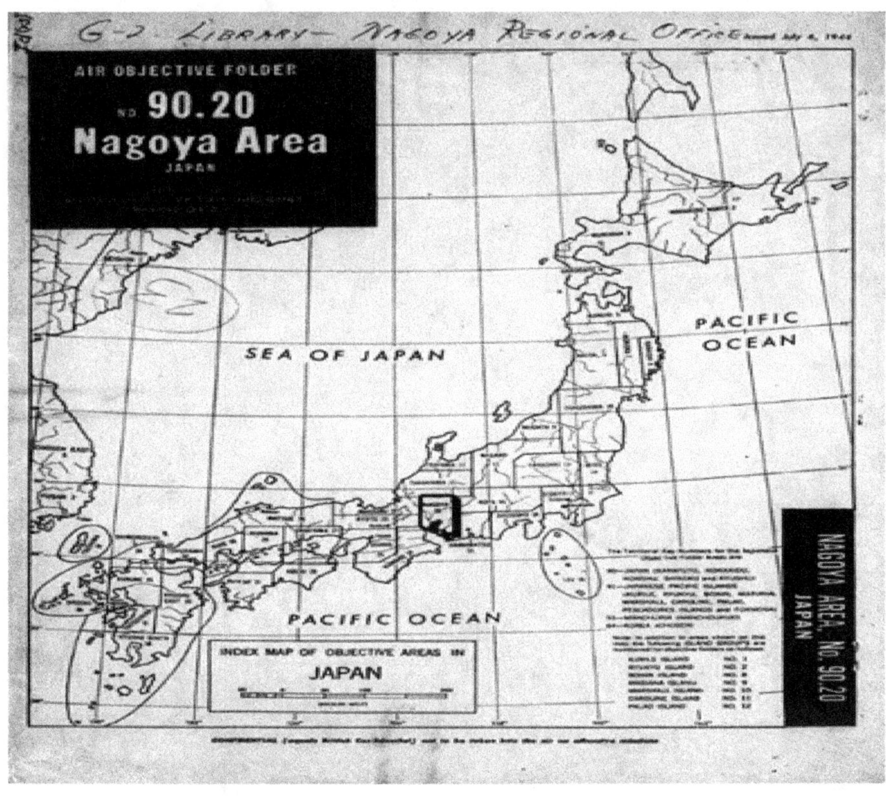

Kuana (Kuwana) in the Nagoya Area
(commons.widimedia.org)

ERNIE PYLE

Ernie Pyle

(Microsoft Bing)

Ernest Taylor Pyle was a Pulitzer Prize–winning American journalist and war correspondent who is best known for his stories about ordinary American soldiers during World War II

Born: Taylor Pyle, August 03, 1900, Dana, Indiana

Died: 18, 1945, Iejima, Okinawa Prefecture, Empire of Japan

Cause of death: Killed in action

PILOTS ADORE CRAMPED B-29

Ernie Pyle – In the Mariana Islands

The B-29 is unquestionably a wonderful airplane. Outside of the famous old Douglas DC-3 workhorse, I've never heard pilots so unanimous in their praise of an airplane.

I took my first ride in one the other day. No, I didn't go on a mission to Japan. We've been through all that before. I don't believe in people going on missions unless they have to. And as before, the pilots here all agreed with me; but I went along on a little practice bombing trip of an hour and a half. The pilot was Maj. Gerald Robinson, who lives in our hut.

I sat on a box between the pilots, both on the takeoff and for the landing, and as much as I've flown, that was still a thrill. These islands are all relatively small, and you're no sooner off the ground than you're out over water, and that feels funny.

If the air is a little rough, it gives you a very odd sensation sitting way up there in the nose. For the B-29 is so big that, instead of bumping or dropping, the nose has a "willowy" motion, sort of like sitting out on the end of a green limb when it's swaying around.

The B-29 carries a crew of 11. Some of them sit up in the cockpit and the compartment just behind it. Some others sit in a compartment near the tail. The tail gunner sits all alone, way back there in the lonely tail turret.

The body of the B-29 is so taken up with gas tanks and bomb racks that there's normally no way to get from front to rear compartments. So the manufacturers solved that by building a tunnel into the plane, right along the rooftop.

The tunnel is round, just big enough to crawl in on your hands and knees, and is padded with blue cloth. It's more like 30 feet long, and the crew members crawl back and forth through it all the time. Maj. Russ Cheever reported that he accomplished the impossible the other day by turning around in the tunnel. On missions some of the crew go back in the tunnel and sleep for an hour or so, but a lot of them can't stand to do that. They say they get claustrophobia.

There used to be some sleeping bunks on the B-29, but they've been taken out, and now there's hardly even room to lie down on the floor. A fellow does get sleepy on a 14-hour mission. Most of the pilots take naps in the seats. One pilot I know turned the plane over to his co-pilot and went back to the tunnel for a "a little nap" and didn't return for six hours, just before they hit the coast of Japan. They laughingly say he goes to sleep before he gets his wheels up.

The B-29 is a very stable plane and hardly anybody ever gets sick even in rough weather. The boys smoke in the plane, and the mess hall gives them a small lunch of sandwiches, oranges, and cookies to eat on the way. On mission days all flying crewmen, even those not going on the mission, get all the fried eggs they want for breakfast. That's the only day they have eggs.

The crewmen wear their regular clothes on missions, usually coveralls. They don't like to wear heavy fleece-lined clothes and all that bulky gear, because the cabin is heated. They do slip on their heavy steel "flak vests" as they approach the target. They don't have to wear oxygen masks except when they're over the target, for the cabin is sealed and "pressurized" – simulating a constant altitude of 8,000 feet.

Once in a great while one of the plexiglass "blisters" where the gunners sit will blow out from the strong pressure inside, and then everybody better grab his oxygen mask in a hurry. The crew always wear the oxygen mask over the target, for a shell through the place "depressurizes" the cabin instantly, and they'd pass out.

The boys speak frequently of the unbelievably high winds they hit at high altitudes over Japan. It's nothing unusual to have a 150-mile an hour wind, and my nephew, Jack Bales, said that one day his plane hit a wind of 250 miles an hour.

Another thing that puzzles and amuses the boys is that often they'll pick up news on their radios, when still only halfway home, that their bombing mission has been announced in Washington. Thus all the world knows about it, but they've still got a thousand miles of ocean to cross before it's finished. Science, she is wonderful.

(9th Bombardment Group (VH) History, p. 168)

B-29S TAKE OFF FOR TOKYO

Ernie Pyle – In the Marianas

I've always felt the great 300-mile auto race at Indianapolis to be the most intriguing event – in terms of human suspense – that I've known. The start of a B-29 mission to Tokyo, from the spectator's standpoint, is almost a duplicate of the Indianapolis race.

On mission day people are out early to see the start. Soldiers in groups sit on favorite high spots around the field – on tops of buildings, on tops of bulldozers along the runway, on mounds that give a better view – and even a few bold souls stand at the very end of the runway to snap amateur pictures as the thundering planes pass just over their heads. As the planes taxi out, it is just like cars at Indianapolis leaving their pits to line up for the start. You wave farewell to your own special friends, and then get as fast as you can to your own favorite spot to watch the spectacle.

My nephew, Lt. Jack Bales, wasn't on this mission, so we drove in a jeep to the far end of the runway, and parked on a raised place alongside it, at a point where the planes better be in the air by that time – or else. "If a plane starts wheeling off the runway," Jack said, "we gotta run like hell."

Most of the planes would be in the air long before they reached us. But a few either had trouble getting off, or else their pilots were holding them down, for they just barely raised in the last few feet of runway, and the amateur photographers down there hit the dirt so hard we had to laugh. The planes were staggering just a little as they took off. The spacing between them was perfect. There was never a blank spot, never a delay. When you turned from seeing one safely off the ground, here would be the next one coming down the runway.

These Mariana Islands are so small that any plane taking off is out over the water within a few seconds. It is a goose-fleshy sensation to see a place clear the bluff by a mere few feet, and then sink out of sight toward the water. This is because the pilots nose down a little to get more flying speed. Pretty soon you see them come up into sight again.

There are no accidents at the start of our mission, but not all the planes did get off. Two were canceled on the ground before starting. Two ran halfway down the airstrip, then cut the power and came rolling off to the side, just like burned out cars at Indianapolis. One of them had locked brakes and was just barely able to pull itself off the airstrip and out of the way. He stayed there alongside the runway as all the others roared past him, seeming, from our position, almost to lock wings with him as they passed.

Finally, they were all in the air, formed into flights, and vanished into the swallowing sky from which some would never return.

I had the same feeling watching the takeoff that I used to have before the start of Indianapolis. Here were a certain number of cars and men. Some of them you knew. They had built and trained for weeks for this day. At last the time had come. And in a few hours of desperate living, everything would be changed. You knew that within a few hours some would be glorious in victory, some would be defected in failures, some would be colorless "also rans," and some – very probably – would be dead.

And that's the way you feel when the B-29s start out. It is just up to fate. In 15 hours they will be back – those who are coming back. But you cannot know ahead of time who it will be.

(9th Bombardment Group (VH) History page, 164)

TRIBUTE TO PAUL M. KERR

Russell's youngest brother, Paul Kerr, also served in WW II. He was a co-pilot and was killed in action over Austria.

Paul M. Kerr was born on October 10, 1920 in Westminster, Ohio to George W. and Goldie Maybell Montague Kerr. Both the US Censuses 1930 and 1940 show the family residing in Auglaize, Ohio..

Kerr enlisted at Fort Benjamin Harrison, Indiana on January 8, 1942 as a private in the Army Air Forces. He was selected for flight duty, and subsequently trained as a pilot. He entered pilot training on March 13, 1943, and received training at both Arcadia, Florida and Greenwood, Mississippi before graduating on January 7, 1944.

He was awarded wings, commissioned, and sent overseas in 1944 to a bomber unit in Italy. There, he flew at least 5 missions.

On July 26, he was tasked as part of a crew to bomb the aircraft engine plant at Weiner-Neudorf, Austria. Weather conditions worsened as the flight progressed, and a Recall was issued. The planes of the 301st Bomb Group did not receive that call, but the fighter escort did, and left.

The unprotected bombers continued to the target area where they were attacked by numerous German fighters. At least 11 of the 38 plane formation were shot down. Kerr's plane was raked from nose to tail by machine gun and cannon fire which killed several crew members at their stations. The aircraft was riddled with holes, and soon crashed near Strallegg, Austria.

Only two crew members survived, and they were captured by enemy troops. The dead were recovered and buried locally. After the war, they were retrieved and moved to various cemeteries. Lt Kerr now lies in the Westminster Salem Cemetery in Westminster, Ohio.

Comments/Citation

Lt Paul M. Kerr was acting as co-pilot on B-17G # 44-6168, not named, assigned to the 32nd Bomb Squadron.

Missing Air Crew Report 7142 was issued, although the copy is faint and redacted in part. No details are given concerning the loss. Mission loading lists show the crew as:

1 Lt Ralph C. Delonney p

2 Lt Paul M. Kerr c-p

2 Lt Bobbie L. Massey nav

2 Lt Jack S. Kuhn bomb

SSgt Gilbert J. Chesney eng/tt gun

TSgt Joseph K. Salasek r/o

SSgt George Demos btg

SSgt Eugene H. Anderson wg

SSgt Melvin K. Stark wg

SSgt Roscoe G. Fulton tail gun

Ranks and grades as of mission date.

In the loading list, the pilot's name is spelled "Delloney," and the navigator's name is spelled "Bobbie." All other sources use "Delonnay" and "Bobby."

(Together We Served)

KERR FAMILY

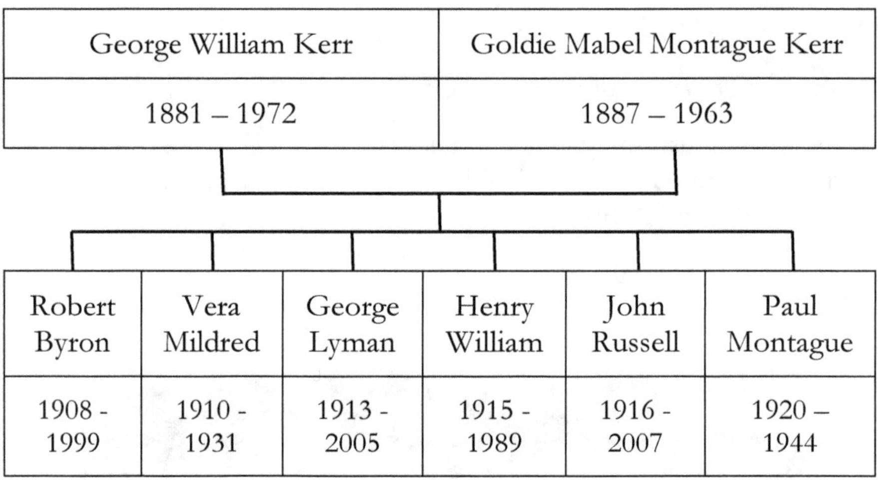

John Russell Kerr	Arnita Ruth (Baier) Kerr
1916 – 2007	1919 - 2000

Ronda Lou Showalter	John Kerr
1942 -	1947- 2010

Robert Byron Kerr		Bernice (Emlich) Kerr	
1908 – 1999		1910 - 1950	
Georgianna Armstrong	Marcella (Sally) (Hamaker) Dubiel	Linda Garrettson	Pamela Atkinson
1930 - 1998	1933 -2015	1947 – 1994	1950 - 2014

These pictures of Fifi were taken by John A. Manera at the 2023 Willow Run Air Show in Ypsilanti, Michigan. This is one of the last two B-29 Superfortresses flying today. One can even reserve a seat for a flight!

Learn more about Fifi at https://www.cafb29b24.org/